101

Ways the Before Bedtime

Paul Mason

CW00866263

CONTENTS

Sending Out an S.O.S   2

Watch Out For Flying Tomatoes   4

Sprinkle Worm Wee on Your Food   6

Eat Less Cow!   8

Make Friends With a Spider   10

Wear Fewer Clothes   12

Make Your Granny Happy   14

Don't Be a Standby Sucker   16

Waste Not, Want Not   18

Make a Monstrous Sock   20

See the World by Bike!   22

Love a Library   24

Get Toilet Trained   26

Be a Role Model   28

Think Differently   30

Glossary and Index   32

SENDING OUT AN

Planet Earth is an amazing place. Just look around at the plants and animals you can see. But Earth is in danger. Why? Well, because of us. Humans are always doing things that aren't good for the planet.

What's the problem?

Global warming is what we call the rise in the world's temperature. That might *sound* like a good thing, but even the smallest rise in temperature can have *big* effects on our planet.

Global warming causes:

- rising sea levels, which are bad for coastal areas

- changes in our weather, like more extreme storms

- less food because some of the world's farmland is becoming too dry to grow things.

Sun

How global warming happens

1. Burning **fossil fuels** like coal and oil releases **greenhouse gases**.

2. Greenhouse gases reach the **atmosphere**.

atmosphere

4. Heat is reflected back towards Earth.

3. Greenhouse gases trap heat.

Earth

Can we save the world?

Earth has a lot of resources like water, wood, food and fossil fuels. These are very important to us, but we are using them up too quickly and they may not last.

Sounds scary, doesn't it? But don't worry! You can help to save the world – one small step at a time. Here are 101 ways how ...

What can I do?

1 Start now

All you have to do is to try one idea from this book before you go to bed today. What are you waiting for?

Top Tip!
This book is special - you can start reading wherever you want. So why not start in the middle?

2 WATCH OUT FOR THE FLYING TOMATOES

Imagine a tasty tomato. (No saying "Yuck!") Would you guess that you could save the world by eating that tomato in August instead of in January? Well, you can!

How can eating tomatoes save the planet?

In January, tomatoes won't grow outside in the UK. But they *will* grow in hot places like Africa. Then they're flown to the UK to be sold. This is *bad* because:

- they travel a long way, which burns lots of fossil fuel
- aeroplanes release greenhouse gases high up in the atmosphere where they do the most harm!

In the summer, tomatoes grow well outside in the UK, so why not grow your own?

FAST FACT
Food from far away is often grown in poor countries and bought cheaply.

2. Put soil in a clean yoghurt pot. Push the seed in and cover with soil.

1. Collect seeds from a tomato and dry them.

Top Tip!

Seeds from a tomato grown in the UK will grow *better* than those from another country.

3. Water regularly and wait ...

4. Soon your tomato plant will start to grow!

3 Grow your own food
Try using other seeds. What else can you grow?

4 Eat at the right time
Encourage your parents to buy seasonal fruit and vegetables.

5 Gather free food
Take a grown-up **foraging**. In autumn the hedges are full of blackberries.

6 Talk food at school
Try to persuade your head teacher that more school food should come from nearby.

7 Persuade your parents
Go shopping and help your parents look for food that is grown nearby.

8 Use leftovers
Cut the amount of food waste in your house by using leftovers to make new meals.

9 Choose farm food
Look for a farmers' market near you and buy locally-grown food.

10 Wrap it up
Instead of wrapping sandwiches in foil or cling-film, use a plastic lunch box.

11 SPRINKLE WORM WEE ON YOUR FOOD

In the UK, people throw away over 30% of the fresh food they buy. What a waste! Instead, they could feed it to worms and use the worm wee to grow more food.

Why put worm wee on food?

It *does* sound pretty horrid, but you're not actually putting worm wee on your plate! Worms make compost and worm wee by eating waste food. Worm wee is a great **fertiliser**! Put it on your plants to help them grow better.

Make your own worm composter

1. Get a grown-up to put small holes in the bottom and lid of a plastic box.

2. Put the box on small stones in a tray.

3. Put some bedding material in the box.

4. Dig a small hollow in the bedding material. Add some leftover raw food and lots of worms.

5. Collect the worm wee that trickles into the tray.

Why not sprinkle your worm wee on your tomato plant? See idea 2.

worms (ask at your local pet shop)

worm wee

small stones

a plastic tray

6

a plastic box with a lid

leftover raw food

damp bedding material (e.g. shredded newspaper, leaves)

Top Tip!
Feed your worms slowly at first.

12 Don't just use the wee
The compost your worms make at the bottom of the box will help your plants grow too.

13 Crack an egg
Sprinkle egg shells around your plants to stop slugs eating them.

14 Welly pots
Use your old wellies as plant pots. Put some holes in the sides to stop plants becoming waterlogged.

15 Scare the birds
Hang up old CDs in your vegetable patch to scare the birds away.

16 Water without waste
Use a watering can rather than a hose. It uses less water.

17 Clean your plate
Only fill your plate with what you can eat, then there won't be any waste.

18 Recycle a Christmas tree
Most local councils recycle old Christmas trees. Some get chipped. Others are left whole and used to make sand dunes more stable!

19 EAT LESS COW!

Want to know one of the biggest causes of global warming? Cows! Cows trump and burp out methane, which is a greenhouse gas.

Why are there so many cows?

Well, because a lot of people eat beef. If we all ate less beef, there would be fewer cows and fewer cow trumps!

Take the veggie burger challenge!

You will need:

4 cups of chopped mushrooms
1/2 cup of chopped onion
1/3 cup of grated cheese
3/4 cup of breadcrumbs
2/3 cup of oats
2 beaten eggs
salt and pepper
oil
1 grown-up

You could also make sure your vegetables are grown nearby. See idea 7.

FAST FACT
Methane is 25 times worse for the planet than carbon dioxide, which is the greenhouse gas released by burning fossil fuels.

- First find a grown-up to help you.
- Heat a little oil in a pan.
- Fry the mushrooms and onions for about 10 minutes.
- Mix everything together in a bowl.
- Leave for 15 minutes.
- Roll the mixture into balls and press flat.
- Put the burgers in the oven to cook.
- Add some bread and eat!

20 **Choose chicken**
Chickens have a smaller effect on the environment than cows.

21 **Learn to love tofu**
Tofu is meat-free but has lots of the same **nutritional** goodness as meat.

22 **Make your parents happy**
Eat more vegetables!

23 **Go veggie**
Be a vegetarian for the day.

24 **Relax!**
Are you a vegetarian? Then your work here is done.

25 **Learn a recipe**
OK, when I said your work was done, I was fibbing. Teach a friend how to make your favourite vegetarian meal.

26 **Leave out the leather**
Try to wear less leather because most leather comes from cows.

27 MAKE FRIENDS WITH A SPIDER

A problem you might have with your worm composter (see idea 11) is flies. Flies just LOVE compost.

How can spiders help save the world?

There's nothing a spider likes more than eating a load of tasty flies. So the next time you see a spider's web, be friendly and leave it there.

Spiders are an important part of the **food chain.** Without them there would be too many flies, and that would mean plants would not grow as well. But spiders get eaten too. Small birds love a tasty spider for lunch. It works like this:

Spiders eat flies.

Birds eat spiders, other insects, seeds and fruit.

Spiders and birds are also part of other food chains.

The birds poo out the seeds.

Trees are perfect homes for spiders and birds.

The seeds grow up into new plants and trees.

28 Set up a nature area
Put a few logs and twigs together outside so that insects can live there.

29 Plant a tree
Grow a tree from a seed or see how the Woodland Trust can help you.

30 Clean up!
Join a local clean-up group and help clean up an area near you.

31 Build a bird a home
Ask a grown-up to help you make a cosy nest box for your local birds.

32 Don't drop it
Help the animals near your home by putting litter in bins, so they don't eat anything dangerous or get caught in the rubbish.

33 Watch it!
Take a look outside and see which animals you can spot. Are they using your nature area or bird box? See ideas 28 and 31.

FAST FACT
Trees remove greenhouse gases from the air and make oxygen for us to breathe.

34 WEAR FEWER CLOTHES

No, this doesn't mean you have to walk around in your underpants to save the world! It really means 'have fewer clothes in your wardrobe.' But hang on – how can that help?

How do clothes affect the world?

Everyone has a cotton T-shirt in their wardrobe. But have you ever thought about what happens before that T-shirt ends up with you?

> ### Growing the cotton
> Firstly, chemicals are used to grow and make cotton, which can be bad for the environment.

> ### T-shirts do a lot of travelling ...
> The cotton has to go from the field to the mill and then to the factory to be made into a T-shirt.

> ### ... and then travel some more!
> Even worse than that – many T-shirts are sold far from where they were made. You know what that means: **longer journeys = more greenhouse gases.**

So why not just have a couple of T-shirts you love rather than lots? See? Wear fewer clothes, and save the world!

FAST FACT
The chemicals used to grow and make cotton stay in the T-shirt.

Top Tip!
Make sure your mum or dad knows what you're swapping or giving away.

35 Stop growing?
Every now and again, your clothes will get too small. What a waste! But hang on – why not give them to charity?

36 Look at the label
Get your mum or dad to look at the labels and ask them to buy clothes made closer to home.

37 Run a swapshop
Bored with your clothes? Swap them with friends!

38 Check out charity
You don't always have to buy new clothes. See what clothes you can find in a charity shop.

39 Wash less
Not you – your clothes! Some clothes don't need to be washed after every wear. Socks and pants probably do though!

40 Glasses give-away
Give your old glasses to a charity.

41 MAKE YOUR GRANNY HAPPY

Make your granny happy *and* save the world? Sounds impossible, but it can be done. And it only takes a few seconds. On cold days, all you need to do is wear that jumper she knitted you.

How can jumpers save the world?

If your granny doesn't knit, don't worry. You can save the world with *any* jumper. Once you've got that lovely jumper on, you'll remember how warm it is. Then, persuade everyone else in your family to put a jumper on too. Notice anything? You're all really warm! Better turn down the heating.

Why turn off the heating?

Well, the heating in most buildings uses electricity, which is usually made with fossil fuels, or gas, which *is* a fossil fuel.

So every time you turn down the heating, you help save the planet just a little bit.

Gas or electricity used for heating

Fossil fuels burned

Greenhouse gases released

Global warming

Top Tip!
Turning the heating down or off can be difficult. Ask a grown-up to help you!

42 Put on a hat
We lose lots of heat through our heads. Putting on a hat is a fast way to stay warm.

43 Toasty toes
Wear extra-thick socks to keep your toes happy.

44 Keep warm at night
Take a hot-water bottle to bed. If you don't have one, add an extra blanket instead.

45 Ban the draft
Shut doors and windows to keep rooms warm.

46 On the spot
Feeling cold? Try running on the spot. How do you feel now?

47 Hug your sister
It doesn't need to be your sister! Hug a friend or pet and you'll soon feel warm.

48 DON'T BE A STANDBY SUCKER

Who'd have thought you could save the world by flicking a switch? The switch you need is ... the off switch! That's the *real* off switch, not the pretend one otherwise known as 'standby'.

What's wrong with standby?

Lots of people turn things off using a standby button. They're not *really* off, because a little bit of electricity is still being used! Most of this electricity was made by burning fossil fuels. This produces greenhouse gases, which adds to the greenhouse effect. When you *do* turn things off properly, they stop running completely.

less electricity wasted = fewer greenhouse gases

Congratulations! With the flick of a switch you've helped save the world!

Top Tip!

Check with a grown-up before turning things off. Not everything can be turned off. Refrigerators have to stay on all the time!

Poster power
Design a poster to remind people to turn things off.

 Start a 'no TV day'
For one day, switch the TV off and do something else instead.

 Turn off the lights
But do make sure there's no one still in the room first.

 Think fast
Hungry? Don't stand with the fridge door open. Decide what you want and close it fast.

 Be bright
Get your parents to use energy-saving bulbs. They use less energy than other bulbs.

 Summer sun
Dry your hair naturally when the weather is warm instead of using a hairdryer.

Want ideas for your no TV day? See ideas 63 to 69.

WASTE NOT, WANT NOT

'Waste not, want not' means don't throw things away carelessly. Then you won't miss them later. It's the kind of thing your grandad might say! 'Wasting not' is also a good way to help save the world from being buried under a Rubbish Mountain.

The Rubbish Mountain really is a rubbish mountain!

What do we waste?

Every year, we throw away a mountain of rubbish. In one year, British people throw away about:

- 972 million plastic bottles
- 24 million car tyres
- 2 million mobile phones
- 94 thousand old fridges.

Here are three things you can do to stop the Rubbish Mountain growing.

Reduce
Reduce the amount of waste you produce. Try to choose things that have little or no wrapping.

Recycle
If you do have to throw things away, make sure they go in a recycling bin.

Reuse
Try to reuse things instead of throwing them away.

56 Blow your nose

When you get a cold or a sniffle, use a handkerchief and not a tissue.

57 Read your rubbish

Learn the recycling symbols and make sure you're recycling as much as you can.

58 Carry on shopping

The next time you go shopping, use a cloth bag or an old plastic bag.

59 One in, one out

Make someone's day. When you get a new toy, give an old one away.

60 Take care

Look after your things. The fewer things you break, the fewer new things you need.

61 Buy second-hand stuff

It helps reduce waste, and means new things don't need to be made.

62 Learn to fix things

Try fixing something that's broken instead of replacing it.

FAST FACT

The amount of waste the UK produces is increasing by 3% each year.

Want more ideas for reusing things? Go to ideas 79 to 83.

63 MAKE A MONSTROUS SOCK

Quite a lot of what we throw away is actually stuff that could be reused or turned into something else. But not everything you make has to be useful. You can make fun things using old stuff too!

How can sock monsters save the world?

They can't do it by themselves – they're not superheroes! But with your help, they can put your old socks to good use.

You will need:

- 1 sock
- stuffing (old fabric cut up)
- scissors, needle and thread
- 2 buttons

2. Cut down from the toe to make two ears. Sew along the edge of the ears.

1. Turn your sock inside out with the heel facing up.

3. Turn your sock the right way out, stuff then sew up the bottom.

Don't forget to use your sleepy shopping bag when you do idea 7.

Top Tip!
Ask a grown-up before you start cutting things up.

64 Brilliant birthday cards
Cover a piece of card with pictures from magazines, then write your own message inside.

65 Sleepy shopping bag
Add handles to an old pillowcase and make a bag. Decorate it with old buttons or fabric.

66 Old is new
Instead of throwing out old clothes, why not alter them to the style you want?

67 Reuse your old jeans
Use the leg of old jeans as door draught stoppers. Cut off a jean leg, stuff it with old fabric or plastic bags, and sew up both ends.

68 Jam jar holders
Jam jars can hold pens, pennies and much more.

69 Think outside the box
Why don't you look at your rubbish and think of new ways to reuse it?

4. Sew on the buttons to make eyes.

5. Push in the heel and sew to make a mouth.

SEE THE WORLD BY BIKE!

Every time you get in a car to go somewhere, you add to global warming. That's because car engines release a greenhouse gas called carbon dioxide. So, one good way to save the world is ... to stop being driven around in cars!

Bring on the bike

Bikes are *way* better than cars, for loads of reasons. The main one is that they don't cough out greenhouse gases. Oh, and they don't get stuck in traffic jams either!

A bike can take you practically everywhere. The next time you plan to go somewhere, think "Can I go by bike?"

Top Tip!
Remember to wear a helmet and make sure your mum or dad knows where you are going.

FAST FACT
Over 30% of car trips in the UK are less than 3.2km long. Perfect for cycling!

71 Use human power
If you don't have a bike, how about skateboarding, walking or rollerblading?

72 Hop on the train or bus
If it's raining, go by train or bus. They burn less fossil fuel per passenger than cars.

73 The walking bus
Ask your school to start a walking bus if you can't cycle to school.

74 Give someone a lift
If you and your friend are going to the same place, get your mum or dad to give them a lift. That means only one car makes the trip, not two.

75 Wind up the windows
If you *do* travel by car, try not to open the windows too much. Cars run better with the windows closed.

76 Go slow
On long car journeys, ask the driver to travel at 55–65mph. Most cars use less fuel at this speed.

77 Plan a day out
The next time you plan a family trip, go somewhere you can get to by train, by bus or on foot.

78 LOVE A LIBRARY

Help save the world by reading books! As long as they're not brand-new copies, that is. Instead, get them from a library. That way fewer books need to be made!

Recycling paper is good ...

In the UK, over 30% of the recycling from people's homes is paper. It comes from books, newspapers, magazines and **packaging**. It's all taken away and turned into new paper. Recycled paper is much better for the planet than non-recycled paper.

... but using less paper is better

Even recycled paper harms the planet. Making it still produces **pollution** and adds to global warming. So wherever possible, try to use less paper.

Still got unwanted paper? Use it in your worm composter. See idea 11.

79 **Double it**
Use the backs of sheets of paper not just the front.

80 **Start a book group**
Share books with your friends, especially this one!

81 **Resend it**
Re-use envelopes. All you need to do is open the envelope carefully, cover the address with a plain white sticker and you're good to go.

82 **Perfect pad**
Make your own scrap-paper pad. Use it for notes and messages.

83 **Reuse newspapers**
Make your own paper plates. Tear up old newspapers and soak them in water. Then press the paper onto a plate and wait for it to dry. Perfect for using for more craft activities.

84 **New ideas**
While you're riding the bus to the library (see idea 72), maybe you can come up with some other paper-related ways to save the world.

85 **No more mail**
Well, no more junk mail! Make a 'no junk mail' sign for your front door.

86 GET TOILET TRAINED

Want to know one of the world's biggest problems right now? It's a lack of water. All across the world, countries are running out of water. The UK is too!

Why is it happening?

- Humans use more water in their homes than they did in the past.

- The number of people in the world is increasing, but the amount of fresh water stays the same. This means there is less for each person.

- More water is being used in farming and industry than ever before.

How can we change things?

You can help save the world by using less water. One way is to flush the toilet less often at home!

After a wee, don't flush. If people don't like the idea, point out that wee does not cause any harm. Just close the lid. Leaving poo hanging around is very unhealthy though. Always flush that away!

FAST FACT
Every time you flush the toilet, it uses up to 12 litres of water. That's six times as much as a person needs to drink each day!

**If it's yellow,
let it mellow.**

Top Tip!
Not everyone will
like you leaving
a wee in their
toilet, so only do
it if you think
they won't mind.
It's probably
best not to do
this at school!

**If it's brown,
flush it down.**

87 Ban drips!
Dripping taps can waste
up to 90 litres of water
a week!

88 Blow up the toilet
Put a water-filled balloon
into the **cistern** of your
toilet. It saves water with
each flush.

89 Shower power
Showers use less water
than baths, but keep
it quick! A five-minute
power shower can use as
much water as a bath.

90 Please your parents!
Offer to do the washing up,
and fill a bowl instead of
leaving the tap running. This
uses a lot less water!

91 Teeth time
Only turn on the tap to
rinse your toothbrush, or
use a glass of water.

92 BE A ROLE MODEL

Many parents come from a time when no one really bothered much about saving the world. This is not their fault – hardly anyone knew back then that the world *needed* saving!

How can I make a difference?

You *are* different. You have lots of ideas about saving the world. Don't be selfish – share what you know. After all, lots of people acting in the same way can make things a *lot* better.

Spread the word

Why not start with your school? Think about the things you would like to do differently. Speak to your classmates and teachers. Can you spread the word and make a difference?

FAST FACT
When **Earth Day** was first celebrated on 22nd April 1970, just one country took part. By 2010, 175 countries celebrated it.

Top Tip!
Remember to ask before changing anything at school.

SAVE THE WORLD TODAY

I would like:

- O more places to put bikes
- O monthly swap-shops for clothes and toys
- O recycling bins in every class
- O walking buses
- O a 'Get to school without a car' day

95 Get sponsored
Do a sponsored walk, swim or cycle for an environmental charity.

96 Be a green author
Make a 'green' book, like this one, explaining to other children what they can do to help save the world.

97 Change a friend
No, don't swap them! Just persuade one friend to do an activity from this book.

98 Look back
Go through the book. Which activities can you do at school?

99 Green days
Start a 'green' diary. Record all the things you do to help save the world.

93 Hold a waste test
Ask if you can monitor the school's bins before they're collected. Could you reduce the amount of rubbish?

94 Celebrate!
Why not get your school to celebrate Earth Day?

100 THINK DIFFERENTLY

One day a cavewoman looked at her husband dragging a load of firewood back to their cave. "I wonder if there's a better way of doing that?" she thought. A week later – hey presto! Wheels!

How can we change things?

Things only change when someone wonders why things are the way they are – and whether they could be better. Great news – you've already started to think differently by reading this book!

THINGS ONLY CHANGE WHEN SOMEONE WONDERS ...

Why not keep a note of your questions in your green diary? See idea 99.

GLOSSARY

atmosphere layer of gases surrounding a planet

cistern storage tank for water

Earth Day chosen day every year for people to think about looking after Earth

fertiliser substance which makes plants grow better

food chain series of plants and animals in which each one serves as food for the next in the chain

foraging hunting for food

fossil fuels energy resources formed from the remains of plants and animals from millions of years ago, which will eventually run out

global warming increase in the temperature of Earth, which may change weather patterns and affect plants, wildlife and people

greenhouse gases gases that cause global warming

nutritional content in food which helps us to stay healthy

packaging wrapping that goes around things we buy

pollution materials that cause harm to the natural world

INDEX

car travel 22, 23
clothes 12–13
cycling 22
Earth Day 28, 29
energy, saving 14, 16–17
food 4–5, 7, 8–9
food chain 10
foraging 5
global warming 2, 8, 14, 16, 22, 24
greenhouse gases 2, 8, 11, 12, 14, 16, 22
growing plants 4–5, 7, 11
heating, turning down 14–15
libraries 24–25
meat, eating 8–9
nature areas 11
paper, saving 24–25
reduce, reuse, recycle 5, 18–21, 24–25
resources 3
rubbish 11, 18–19, 21, 29
showers 27
sock monsters 20
spiders 10
spreading the word 28–29
swapping and giving away 13, 19
tofu 9
toilets, flushing 26–27
tomatoes 4
travel 22–23
vegetarians 9
veggie burgers 8
warm, keeping 14–15
water, saving 7, 26–27
worm composter 6–7